Also by the Author

LOVING GOD: Statement of Faith
Ethiopia Medical Mission (It helps the next mission)

LOVING GOD:

The Revelation of God,

Volume 1

Belinda Shek-lai Yung BS, BSN, MATS

WESTBOW
PRESS
A DIVISION OF THOMAS NELSON

WestBow Press books may be ordered through booksellers or by contacting:

WestBow Press
A Division of Thomas Nelson
1663 Liberty Drive
Bloomington, IN 47403
www.westbowpress.com
1-(866) 928-1240

ISBN: 978-1-4497-6243-8 (e)
ISBN: 978-1-4497-6242-1 (sc)

Library of Congress Control Number: 2012914102

Printed in the United States of America

WestBow Press rev. date: 08/23/2012

DEDICATION

The LOVING GOD series is dedicated to those who want to know God better, continually walking with Him, who have walked before me, who are walking with me now, who are going to walk after me, in regardless of our walks in different time frame, and who hold this belief, Immanuel (Matthew 1:23). Our spiritual walks are never alone, but always walking with God through the Lord Jesus Christ.

PREFACE

This book, *LOVING GOD: The Revelation of God, Volume 1,* continues the series of the previous book: *LOVING GOD: Statement of Faith,* which is published in April, 2012. Reading the Word of God every day, I receive the understanding of His Word little by little in which it has consecrated my heart, mind, and my soul, as the understanding continually strengthening my walk and faith in God through the Lord Jesus Christ. Every time when I pray in Christ's name, either in my mind or through my lips, I experience God's presence in my midst.

The purpose of this book, *LOVING GOD: The Revelation of God, Volume 1,* is to introduce the only living God on this planet Earth, as He has said in His Word, the everlasting Word that He is the Creator God. This book, according to the Word of God, is written through the lens of other people's lives in the midst of peace, disaster, distress, disappointment, or disease, helping the readers, either believers or non-believers, to remove the fear of false teaching, false doctrine, and of false church, so they can have a better, clear understanding of God and of His revelation to His creature, people. It also helps people to see Him, to experience His presence, and to strengthen the faithful walk that, being guided and protected by the Holy Spirit, never a lonely walk, is always walking with God through the Lord Jesus Christ and His Holy Spirit.

Listening to God's voice, through the reading, meditating, or the hearing of the Word of God, people will have faith in God through the Lord Jesus Christ. Pray that this book continues to help readers to have a more-realistic and more-practical perspective of the living God with a joyful and faithful heart (Philippians 4:4).

TEN COMMANDMENTS

(Exodus 20:1-17)

I. Only worship God the Father, the Creator God.

II. Do not commit idolatry.

III. Do not misapply God's name.

IV. Honor the Sabbath day.

V. Honor your parents.

VI. Do not kill.

VII. Do not commit adultery.

VIII. Do not steal.

IX. Do not testify untruly against your neighbor.

X. Do not covet.

CONTENTS

"The most important one," answered Jesus,
"is this: 'Hear, O Israel, the Lord our God,
the Lord is one. Love the Lord your God
with all your heart and with all your soul
and with all your mind and with all your
strength.'"

(Mark 12:29-30)

LOVING GOD: THE REVELATION OF GOD, VOLUME 1

"God saw all that he had made, and it was very good. And there was evening, and there was morning—the sixth day. Thus the heavens and the earth were completed in all their vast array. By the seventh day God had finished the work he had been doing; so on the seventh day he rested from all his work. And God blessed the seventh day and made it holy, because on it he rested from all the work of creating that he had done" (Genesis 1:31-2:3).

Loving God is the most important, the highest theological goal for all His people, regardless of their physical, mental, social, cultural, economic, academic, political, or racial status. God has expounded Himself through His everlasting Word, the Word of God, to His people.

I.
INTRODUCTION

"In the beginning God created the heavens and the earth" (Genesis 1:1).

The clear sky (Genesis 1:8; Exodus 24:10) is light blue, because of the Sun shining (Deuteronomy 4:19) onto this part of the earth, so we can see the beautiful pastel blue color on the sky, also called stratosphere. Another layer above this stratosphere is called Ozone, which is made by God. Would people ask themselves why the earth needs the ozone layer? Why would our scientists not make the ozone layer out of their laboratories? If they could make it, how could they cover our planet earth? What are the exact ingredients in the Ozone? And, why is the ozone layer so important to our planet Earth?

Now let our eyes look up to the sky again, and it is cloudy (Exodus 14:20). The clouds are thick, dark greyish (Exodus 19:16); the storm is coming (Matthew 16:2-3), and people are going to make preparations to anticipate the coming storm. When a meteorologist addresses the weather reports for today and the next several days, there may be sunshine and dry weather, or there may be tornado warning, because of the confrontations between the cold and warm air pressure. While listening to these reports, people should respond to the reports accordingly and expectantly.

Sometimes we have warm days, we have cold days, and sometimes we have stormy days (Exodus 9:23; Psalm 55:8; Isaiah 29:6). For whatever the weather may be, we know ahead of time. We know how to dress up appropriately according to the weather, though we may sometimes overdress ourselves, then removing the outer layer. The sense that we can feel warm or cold weather is made by God (Genesis 1:14; 3:21).

God called the expanse "sky." And there was evening, and there was morning—the second day. And God said, "Let the water under the sky be gathered to one place, and let dry ground appear." And it was so.

(Genesis 1:8-9)

II.

THE UNIVERSE

"For since the creation of the world God's invisible qualities—his eternal power and divine nature—have been clearly seen, being understood from what has been made, so that men are without excuse" (Romans 1:20).

A clear dark night with no electricity in my area means power outage. Walking out from my apartment to the parking lot, I looked up to the sky, a cloudless night, having counted thousands of stars (Genesis 22:17), just from my naked eyes. Of course, the number is supposed to be much bigger (Deuteronomy 1:10), for the counting is from the human eyes. The stars, in a layman term (Genesis 22:17), are also called the planets in a scientific term; some are so far away, and some are near.

The stars, with different colors, are yellow, orange, blue, red, and white, in different sizes which some are small and some are big. The smallest one is so far away and so difficult to pinpoint from our eyes. The biggest one is so obvious that it is big, and the light is radiated from different angles. A shooting star flies very fast, unbelievable fast, which is less than one second, flying from one corner of the sky to the other corner, with a long tail on its back. What if just one shooting star hit our planet Earth, which had no protective layers, then what would happen to us? And why would those shooting stars have never destroyed the earth?

And when you look up to the sky and see
the sun, the moon and the stars—all the
heavenly array—do not be enticed into
bowing down to them and worshiping
things the LORD your God has apportioned
to all the nations under heaven.

(Deuteronomy 4:19)

The stars, or the planets, up there on the sky, are so far away from us, and we can see them every night after the planet Sun comes down. The stars are walking on the same path again and again, day after day, month after month, and year after year, e.g., the faithful moon (Psalm 89:37). Their loyalty is a good model for our walks with God through the Lord Jesus Christ. If a star, one of the planets, disobeyed the Creator God's instruction, then what would happen to our planet Earth?

The other planets have the planet moon, like the planet Earth, and some planets have more than one moon. Thinking about those moons, we have not seen other moons flowing around randomly, or any moon flying to other planet. For instance, the moon that we see every night is always up there in a cloudless night or a cloudy night. The planet Moon, moving around the earth on its own path, is not going to fly to other planet, e.g., Saturn. Otherwise, we might not have the moon, having no light on earth at night time for which the Sun would have no object, e.g., the moon, to reflect its bright sunlight.

During the day time, the planet Sun dutifully shines on the half of the planet Earth, and during the night time, the other half of the earth only receives the moonlight, being reflected from the sun (Deuteronomy 4:19). Most people on our earth take vacation. What if our moon took vacation, what would happen then? God has revealed His presence to His people, when they appreciate His divine works to His creation, such as having the moonlight when the sun is gone.

For I am convinced that neither death nor
life, neither angels nor demons, neither the
present nor the future, nor any powers,
neither height nor depth, nor anything else
in all creation, will be able to separate us
from the love of God that is in Christ Jesus
our Lord.

(Romans 8:38-39)

III.
THE PLANET EARTH

"Whenever the rainbow appears in the clouds, I will see it and remember the everlasting covenant between God and all living creatures of every kind on the earth. So God said to Noah, "This is the sign of the covenant I have established between me and all life on the earth"" (Genesis 9:16-17).

The planet earth has two poles, called the South Pole and the North Pole, and the earth has gravity, being found by a scientist, who had received the godly wisdom to reveal some of God's creation several centuries ago. Can scientists make the gravity in their laboratories? So far, no one can do it. Why is the gravity so important to our planet Earth? If we did not have the gravity, what would happen to us on earth? Or, we might have the problems to see the traffic lights while we were bouncing here and there. Does our neighboring planet Moon have gravity? The astronauts have proved that the moon has no gravity since 1967, and it is because they have been bouncing here and there on the moon.

The gravity on earth is to protect us and to help us to walk on the ground (Genesis 1:15), so we will not end up bouncing around on the air and bumping each other in the air and on the ground. How is our precious water related to the gravity? Let us go back to the moon again. Having no water, the moon has no gravity. If the moon had only one ocean, would it be able to retain the water when it has no gravity? If the earth had no gravity, when it turned, can we imagine where the water would go? The gravity, being able to hold or to retain the water, is specially created by God, and it can only be found on this planet Earth.

Then God said, "I give you every seed-bearing plant on the face of the whole earth and every tree that has fruit with seed in it. They will be yours for food. And to all the beasts of the earth and all the birds of the air and all the creatures that move on the ground—everything that has the breath of life in it—I give every green plant for food." And it was so.

(Genesis 1:29-30)

Now we are going to do an experiment. One fills up a full glass of water, and the glass itself has no gravity. Hold up the glass of water on one hand, walk very fast for a minute, and then turn the glass upside down. After walking very fast and turning the glass upside down, has any water left in the glass? Thus, where is the water now? The answer is the water, at least, is found on the ground, and there is no more water left in the glass. It is because the glass itself has no gravity, like the planet Moon.

Our oceans, lakes, rivers, and reservoirs have water. If the northern hemisphere turned upside down, the water (Genesis 1:20) filling in the oceans, lakes, rivers, or reservoirs of the northern hemisphere would have spilled all over to the universe, as a result of the turning motion, like the above experiment. But we still have water in our oceans, lakes, rivers, and a reservoir, for our earth has gravity, as a part of God's design (Genesis 1).

Back in the seventies, when the U.S.A. astronauts, landing on the planet Moon and wearing the heavy clothing with a big round helmet and with the tubing connecting on the back, had a big solid "backpack" on their back, they were bouncing around here and there on the moon. However, people on earth do not bounce here and there, and they are glad that they do not need to wear the astronauts' clothing or to use their gears on earth, for the earth has gravity, as it has shown in the book of Genesis. What if the earth had no gravity, we might be able to bounce from San Diego to New York City, like the moon-walking astronauts, and we might save the travelling cost for a free bouncing-ride; then the mountain-high safety and survival issues would come up to challenge all living animals, plants, and the environment on this planet Earth, such as retaining water (Genesis 1:20).

They will be exposed to the sun and the
moon and all the stars of the heavens, which
they have loved and served and which they
have followed and consulted and worshiped.
They will not be gathered up or buried, but
will be like refuse lying on the ground.

(Jeremiah 8:2)

The earth is turning and moving. If the earth had no gravity, the water on earth was like the water in the glass, and the water on earth would end up into the universe. The planet Earth might then be as dry as the surface of the moon. The gravity is to keep the water not flying, nor flowing, out from the earth, and without God's design, the earth could be like the other dry planets, such as the moon (Psalm 89:37). This is one of the main reasons that I do not want to drive on the moon, for it is going to be a bumpy ride. God has created the earth for His creatures, e.g., humans and plants. It is for us to acknowledge His presence, to appreciate His creation, and to love and to respect His creatures, such as human beings, who are either believers or non-believers.

The ozone layer protects the earth from all flying materials, such as the radioactive molecular particles from the Sun. Have people found the ozone layer in any scientific laboratory? Or, can the scientists have the ability to repair the ozone layer, such as flying up onto the space to patch up the ozone holes? Have any astronauts found any ozone layer on any other planets? At least, they cannot find the ozone layer on our neighboring planet Moon. What if the scientists could make the ozone layer, but how could they implement the ozone layer to cover the whole earth? Looking back to the earth from the moon, the astronauts find the earth is very small, like an ornament hanging on the Christmas tree.

Father, I want those you have given me
to be with me where I am, and to see my
glory, the glory you have given me because
you loved me before the creation of the
world.

(John 17:24)

The ozone layer is very important to His creatures, e.g., all living animals and plants, on earth (Genesis 1). Its vitality is far more than what people can understand or anticipate. Its presence is our protection. If there was no ozone layer, God's creatures would not have survived today. There are explosions in the universe, and sometimes the explosion may give birth to new stars. The earth has never been affected by any kind of explosion, including the explosion in the Sun, which is called the solar storm. The presence of the ozone layer has become our protection for such kinds of cosmic events in our universe.

The ozone layer protects us from the solar radiation, and sometimes the beautiful colorful lights, such as green, red, pink, purple, or blue, on the sky may indicate that our sky has some holes in the ozone layer. The lights are colorful, but they tell us the problem of the ozone layer. If the ozone layer has not made by any scientist or any saint, then who can make the ozone layer? Why can the ozone layer only be found on the planet earth? If God had not made the ozone layer to protect the earth, we would have been gone already. Besides, the moon looks so ugly, with dry ground, a hole here and there, no green pasture, no bluish green oceans, no green plants, and with no high mountain, for it has no ozone layer to protect itself (Genesis 1-2).

By wisdom the LORD laid the earth's
foundations, by understanding he set the
heavens in place; by his knowledge the
deeps were divided, and the clouds let drop
the dew.

(Proverbs 3:19-20)

The ozone layer has been existed since people exist, its presence having been found by a scientist several decades ago, and the scientists have started to do research about the environment of our earth, e.g., pollution, global warming, greenhouse gases effects, effects of new currents, ice melting on both poles, and extreme weather. The holes on the ozone layer and the changes of weather are caused by the industrialization and deforestation.

God gives people His wisdom how to be good stewards and stewardesses to take good care of His planet Earth, such as the books of Genesis and Numbers. The adverse side effects from the industrialization and deforestation have affected our environment, and people start to experience the side effects, e.g., the extreme weather pattern, in which they start to blame God. People have forgotten that the Creator God has given His instruction in His Word, the Word of God, to help them to minister the earth, such as the books of Genesis, Exodus, and Deuteronomy.

God has created the heaven and earth (Genesis 1), and the earth is made specifically for His creatures (Genesis 2). What make people think that God would turn around to destroy His people and His planet earth after He specifically designs His planet earth for His creatures? God loves His creations and He loves people before they love Him (1 John 4:19). God gives His instructions to people of how to manage His earth, such as the usage of the land in the books of Leviticus and Jeremiah. His presence on earth is so obvious that one cannot deny His divine wisdom (Genesis 1-2). Have people thought about how come they have rice, pasta, or bread to eat?

And the LORD God made all kinds of trees
grow out of the ground—trees that were
pleasing to the eye and good for food. In the
middle of the garden were the tree of life
and the tree of the knowledge of
good and evil.

(Genesis 2:9)

Moreover, messing up the environment, which is the planet Earth, people blamed God for their problems in which they have been reluctant to anticipate finding the solutions for the problems. However, God has alternatives to which He has given different kind of wisdom to different people, who have used His wisdom to solve the earthly problems, which can be prevented and will have new preventive measures to prevent future loss. It is not that people on earth would not have the problems, but instead, they should trust God's instructions to keep them safe and to help them to live in healthy manners on this planet Earth.

Use the silver to buy whatever you like:
cattle, sheep, wine or other fermented drink,
or anything you wish. Then you and your
household shall eat there in the presence of
the LORD your God and rejoice.

(Deuteronomy 14:26)

IV.
THE CREATURES

"It will be a sign between me and the Israelites forever, for in six days the LORD made the heavens and the earth, and on the seventh day he abstained from work and rested" (Exodus 31:17).

God is the Creator God (Genesis 1:1), creating human beings, plants, and animals on this earth. In the midst of our earth, we breathe in and breathe out. Can we breathe in any air or any concentration of air? The answer is "No." People can only breathe in and breathe out in a very specific concentration of air. What if the astronauts wore no helmet during the space-walk, what would happen then? And if breathing in too much of one kind of airs, such as carbon dioxide, one may have serious health trouble, called hypercapnia, which means too much carbon dioxide in the blood. If people breathe in the very low concentration of oxygen, e.g., 84% of the oxygen, they will get sick immediately, and the condition is called hypoxia that means too low of the oxygen in the blood.

The air that we breathe in and out has to be exact measures to keep us alive and healthy. The content of the air for our respiratory system is made by God. Can the plants have our respiratory system? The plants have their holes on their surfaces, and their own respiratory systems are also specially made by God. Some of the plants do not need oxygen at all. The breathing systems of human beings and of plants cannot be mixed up, and both systems are uniquely designed by God. If the plants disobeyed God's instructions, rather choosing to have human breathing system, what would happen then?

God is the Creator God (1 Peter 4:19), setting up the rules and regulations for His creatures to survive and to live safely and healthy, such as the books of Numbers and Leviticus. If there were no God, what would the human beings be like? People might all look like the plants, and they had no complaints at all. But, God has made people into His image to have life; and people, the human beings, are all made from His image (1 Corinthians 11:7; Colossians 1:15).

"The god of this age has blinded the minds
of unbelievers, so that they cannot see the
light of the gospel of the glory of Christ,
who is the image of God."

(2 Corinthians 4:4)

Walking on the ground, people have the gravity, being made by God, from the center of the earth. God has made people into His image in which people have the spiritual senses (Genesis 2:7) of hearing, seeing, feeling, speaking, reasoning, and of discerning, though they may be short or tall, may be dark skin or light skin, may be female or male, may be young or old, or may be from the East or the West, but they have the images of God (Colossians 3:10). Thus, God is the Creator God (Genesis 1:1).

The wisdom that we have is given from God, as we continually seek Him (Matthew 6:33; Luke 11:9). God gives people with different kinds of talent and of wisdom, to do good and to take good care of His planet Earth, using neither their powers to manipulate others nor their authorities to destroy others that they dislike. People are meant to do good to each other, to behave in a good manner, and to be a good citizen of the planet Earth. The storm (Exodus 9:23; Ezekiel 13:11) and flooding (Genesis 8:2; 1 King 18:45) cannot separate people from their God, and people should not blame Him either.

Having expounded His presence in His creation and His Word, God does not force anyone to become His believers (Matthew 11:15; Luke 8:8), instead of giving His creatures freedom to choose. People's choosing to obey or disobey His commandments holds them accountable for their own choice. Has God forced people to become His believers? Has God blamed people for not obeying His commandments? When people have made bad choice, yielding bad consequence, can they blame God for their bad decision?

Our responses are what that count. Neither our responses can be forced nor coaxed, by any force or by any human being, to accept God as their personal God (1 Chronicles 29:3; Romans 3:30) or to accept Lord Jesus Christ as their personal Savior (1 Timothy 4:10). Our responses to Him have to be genuine, which is according to our own will. The Creator God has provided different kind of wisdom to different people, and some may be teachers, some may be doctors, some may be scientists, or some may be janitors. Some are good people, good citizens, good neighbors, or good colleagues. But some are bad people, and they do evil things to which they disobey God's commandments (Hebrews 3:18; 1 Peter 3:20). Their acts may also be crimes in our society. For whatever things are not aligned to His commandments, they alienate from Him. God has created people from their mother's womb, and how can this God come back to destroy them to whom He has created?

All of us also lived among them at one time,
gratifying the cravings of our sinful nature
and following its desires and thoughts.
Like the rest, we were by nature objects of
wrath. But because of his great love for us,
God, who is rich in mercy, made us alive
with Christ even when we were dead in
transgressions—it is by grace you
have been saved.

(Ephesians 2:3-5)

†

Different kinds of Satan, e.g., Matthew 4:10 and Mark 8:33, or evil doings, such as sexually immorality, stealing, slandering from making false accusation, kidnapping, drunk-driving, destroying other's credit, killing, or idolatry (Romans 1:18-32), really happen in our midst, and we do not know them. Thus, some of them become crimes. If the authority, such as the policemen, has caught those sinners, or criminals in a legalistic view, the sinners may end up in jail under a court of justice, as such that has been expounded in the Ten Commandments, God's general moral instructions. If one saw a crime was in the progress, what would one respond? The safe and normal response is: one calls the "911" and waits for the policemen, so both the victim and the individual, who has called the "911," may be protected by the response.

The evil things do happen, such as in Genesis 4:3-11, but they are not caused by God. For instance, Hitler rounded up the Jews, or legally kidnapping children, who may be young or old, and the other nations knew what had happened to the Jews there. This example illustrates the individual, like Hitler, who has chosen to do bad things against God's humanity and civilization. None of the God's commandments, e.g., the Ten Commandments (Deuteronomy 5) or the Great Commission Commandment (Matthew 28:18-20), has given people a right to kill or to destroy anyone, and it is simply not God's doing, nor His will. As Hitler continued his obnoxious invasion in Europe, his ambition had stirred up the attacks from other nations. Finally Hitler killed himself to close the chapter of his cruel, brutal ambition, and as the result of his death, Jews have finally saved.

Satan sometimes adds pressure, e.g., starving or death threat, to people to force them to do bad things against God's will. The sinful nature, or Satan's nature, having the complicated view, to which it is not a black and white picture, is still about the people's response and their responsive time to a problem. The complexity of making a decision, either for God or against Him, is all depended upon what kinds of the values of those decision-makers have. Thus our responses do change things around. God gives His wisdom to us, and we should not blame Him when things have gone wrong, e.g., disaster or distress.

The Spirit of the LORD will rest on him—
the Spirit of wisdom and of understanding,
the Spirit of counsel and of power, the Spirit
of knowledge and of the fear of the LORD

(Isaiah 11:2)

✝

The weather man said the storm was coming, and what should people do? Is the stormy weather a new problem on earth? No. For instance, different kind of storms has happened in other nations, e.g., tornado (Joel 2:10), hail (Joshua 10:11), rain (2 Samuel 22:12), or hurricane (Exodus 9:23-24; Psalm 18:11), and our nation has experienced the same kinds of storms from the past, even before our nation was born in the eighteenth century. Then, why would people blame God for the stormy weather in the twenty-first century? And when people would not even choose Him as their personal God, God has never blamed them at all during all these times.

God is so quiet to wait for them to return. Still it comes down to our responses to Him. God has said that whichever decision people make, people make it to the glory of God (1 Cor. 10:31). Besides, He has not made any commandments or laws, such as the Ten Commandments, to anyone to get rid of other, to destroy other, or to kill other.

Turning our eyes back to God's creations, our basic needs in the Eden garden (Genesis 1-2) have been made by God. Being in our midst, God continually helps us to reconcile with Him (Romans 5:11; 2 Corinthians 5:18). Having made air for us to breathe, He has made the Holy Spirit available for people, who choose to have the spiritual breathing. Both kinds of airs, the breathing air (Genesis 1:26; 2:7) and the spiritual air (Genesis 1:2; John 14:26), are vital to us; the former is related to the physical and biological needs, and the latter is related to the spiritual needs (Mark 1:8; 1 Thessalonians 1:5).

The air that we breathe is the basic need, and we all have to have it. The spiritual air, the Holy Spirit, is only given to those who choose to accept God as their personal God and the Lord Jesus Christ as their personal Savior. Or, the other way to say, God gives people freedom to choose the spiritual air. The Holy Spirit is only given to those who respond to Him (Mark 1:8; John 14:26). Our response, either accepting God or rejecting Him, is the crucial determination of receiving the gifts of the Holy Spirit (Galatians 5:22-23).

In the presence of God and of Christ Jesus,
who will judge the living and the dead, and
in view of his appearing and his kingdom,
I give you this charge: Preach the Word;
be prepared in season and out of season;
correct, rebuke and encourage—with
great patience and careful instruction.

(2 Timothy 4:1-2)

When God makes people, people are not just the human beings, who are assigned by God to take good care of His planet earth but also the temples of the Holy Spirit, which are directly made by Him, after reconciling with Him (2 Corinthians 5:18). The Lord Jesus Christ has warned people not to mess up His temples (Matthew 21:12-17), for the temples are the temples of the Holy Spirit, and we are that temples (1 Corinthians 3:16-17). However, if people refuse to allow God to cleanse their temples, then the temples would be infested by all kinds of sin, such as slandering, abusing, committing adulterous acts, kidnapping, hurting others, stealing, lying, cheating, or killing. Similarly, when one's home is filled with trash, one will clean out the trash; then one's home becomes a clean, habitable home again. Thus, if His temple is dirty, the temple will be cleansed by the Word of God in the name of Lord Jesus Christ. No human power will be and would be able to cleanse it, only by the power of God (Psalm 51:10; John 15:3).

Maintenance of His temple, which is the calling and the responsibility of His believers (John 14:15), is to make sure the temple in a non-infested situation or in a healthy manner, spiritually speaking (Hebrews 10:22). To ensure His church following His rules and regulations, e.g., 1 Timothy 2-5, not walking away from Him, not pushing His Word aside or out from His Sanctuary, and not yielding to the worldly treasures (Ephesians 6:10-18), such as greediness, committing sexually immorality, preaching false doctrine, racism, or forcing people committing fornication, are the responsibilities of His people (Matthew 28:18-20; Acts 18:11; 1 Timothy 4:13).

If they have escaped the corruption of the
world by knowing our Lord and Savior Jesus
Christ and are again entangled in it and
overcome, they are worse off at the end than
they were at the beginning.

(2 Peter 2:20)

V.
GOD'S INSTRUCTIONS

"In the beginning was the Word, and the Word was with God, and the Word was God. He was with God in the beginning. Through him all things were made; without him nothing was made that has been made" (John 1:1-3).

The Word of God, the Scriptures (Matthew 21:42; Luke 24:45), having been existed thousands and thousands years ago, is written for keeping His creatures safe, being the measures to protect His creation, such as human beings, animals, or plants. For instance, having spent six days to create heaven and earth (Genesis 1), God has made sure human beings to have air to breathe, to have light to see, to have food to eat . . . and to have water to drink, before He made our ancestors, Adam and Eve (Genesis 1-2). If God made human beings first, how would the sequences of creating heaven and earth have affected their lives, such as the basic need of air? Otherwise, they would not have air to breathe if they were made first.

The careful divine planning from our Creator God is much more than meeting our biological and physical needs but also the spiritual needs. His planning is very calculable and sophisticated, as in the Old Testament and the New Testament. His creation has demonstrated His divine wisdom that we can neither comprehend nor understand all of His wisdom. After creating the heaven and earth, God has given His instructions to Adam and Eve (Genesis 1-2), and both of them were turning around against Him (Genesis 3). They, instead, choosing the Satan's direction (Genesis 3), have deceived their Creator God (Genesis 3:14-24). However, God has never given up His creatures, even though Satan has tried to snatch His people away from Him (1 Timothy 5:11; 2 John 7).

Continually teaching His chosen ones, such as prophets, teachers, kings, judges, and apostles, to teach His people, e.g., Acts 18:11, God has lastly sent His only Son to die on the cross and to pay for people's sins once for all (Romans 6:10; Hebrews 7:27), for He has realized the weakness and wantonness of His people (1 Timothy 5:11), including His own covenanted people, the Israelites. However, He never gives up His creatures, as continually revealing His way to people.

Now we who have believed enter that rest, just as God has said, "So I declared on oath in my anger, 'They shall never enter my rest.'" And yet his work has been finished since the creation of the world.

(Hebrews 4:3)

God's Word, or the Scriptures, including instructions, warnings, teachings, commandments, rewards, and the prophecies, is for His creatures to read and to know Him (Joshua 23:6-8; Romans 16:25-27). He does not and will not force anyone to accept Him or to obey His commandments. The responsibility of taking good care of His planet earth is His creatures, people, since they are the highest animal, in the midst of the animal kingdom (Genesis 1:26-28). Despite of His clear instructions of how to taking care things on earth and in the spiritual realm, have people heard Him? When the things are gone wrong, it is because people refuse to follow God's manual, which is God's Word. It is not because God would like to destroy His creatures. People are always creatures, being part of His creation. The Creator God is always their God (John 10:30; Galatians 3:28), and that will not have another way around to change their status, as His creatures (Genesis 2), or any promotion of His people to become gods or goddesses.

Things are gone wrong, such as diseases (Matthew 4:23), disappointments (Luke 18:23), distress (Romans 2:9), or disasters (Joshua 10:11). People's blaming attitude is usually pointing to God, or some may blame His believers. Some may even change their religion from Christian to a non-Christian religion. Some may just hate God for their suffering from the false practice, e.g., abuse, due to the false teaching, false preaching, false doctrine, or the false church. Before blaming God and His Word, people have forgotten to re-study His Word or to re-examine themselves.

Creating human beings, God will not and would not create some rules, laws, regulations, or some teachings to abuse or to destroy His creatures, to whom He loves and creates (Genesis 1:26-27; Hebrews 9:12, 26). God has no commandment to abuse, to hurt, to kill, or to destroy His own creatures. Continually, people have to study His instructions, for the instructions are actually to protect them, to preserve the integrity and dignity of His humanity, and to defend His temples of the Holy Spirit. Again God has made no commandments, e.g., the Ten Commandments (Deuteronomy 5), whatsoever to destroy His creatures and temples (1 Corinthians 3:16–17), especially to those who have already been initiated by Him and believed in His name (1 John 3:23).

The LORD wrote on these tablets what he
had written before, the Ten Commandments
he had proclaimed to you on the mountain,
out of the fire, on the day of the assembly.
And the LORD gave them to me.

(Deuteronomy 10:4)

Satan and the satanic force have the prideful and stubborn natures, which have caused all the human sufferings and distress. Suffering is not caused by God. For instance, a warning label, on a package of cigarette, has clearly warned smokers not to smoke, and people still choose to smoke and die from the lung cancer due to smoking. Another instance, the people illegally kept the children, called kidnapping, and they were the ones who abused the victims, who harmed them, and who hurt them. The kidnappers are the ones who refuse to release them, and they are the ones to be blamed for the creation of the victims. God has nothing to do with the kidnappers, even though they may say that they were Christians, but they are not (Matthew 7:15; 1 Timothy 6:3; 2 John 7).

True Christians only hear God's voice, His Word, and God has said that only His sheep recognize His voice, which is His instructions (John 10:3). Instead, Satan, wearing wolf's clothing and saying that he was a Christian, refuses to obey God's commandments, and he twists His instructions (Mark 8:33; 1 Timothy 6:3), for he thinks he can sin against God's will, and he says, "God allows me to do . . ." to destroy His creation.

God's Word is to protect us, to help us to discern satanic forces or godly acts, and to defend us in the midst of troubles. The Ten Commandments (Deuteronomy 5) are to help people to immediately discern Satan and God's people. Do not blame God if bad thing happens, for He never does anything against His own creation or Word. Satan has tried to tear down God's temples (1 Corinthians 3:9), which are people (1 Corinthians 3:16-17), and God does not destroy His own creation. Or, if a builder builds his new house, would he burn down his new home?

This is the covenant I will make with the house of Israel after that time, declares the Lord. I will put my laws in their minds and write them on their hearts. I will be their God, and they will be my people.

(Hebrews 8:10)

VI.
HUMAN RESPONSES THROUGHOUT THE HISTORY

"But God turned away and gave them over to the worship of the heavenly bodies. This agrees with what is written in the book of the prophets: "'Did you bring me sacrifices and offerings forty years in the desert, O house of Israel" (Acts 7:42).

God has chosen His people, Israelites, with whom He has made His covenant (Genesis 9:9), but the Israelites have rejected Him (Isaiah 52-53). The Israelites have been against His Begotten Son, Jesus Christ, as their Messiah, who has come from their own race. Israel's history, not having been filled with His glory, instead, have been scattered around. The history has its highlights, such as the famous rescue mission in which Moses has led his people out of Egypt across the Red Sea (Exodus 13:18-22). The rescue mission is obviously protected by God, and it has been proved several thousand years later by the scientists that the Red Sea rescue mission is actually happened at that time.

The Word of God is inerrant, and the Holy Spirit dwells in it. His Word has closed and has sealed thousands and thousands years ago. His Word, or the Scriptures, can be found in a library, a bookstore, a search engine, e.g., Google, a biblical website, e.g., Bible.is, or media, such as audio tapes. His Word, or the Scriptures, has already been translated into thousands of languages, including the dialects, and the translators have become more professional, better equipped, and more experienced than the past.

The Word of God has been available for many centuries, and its existence is not new to many people. People hold responsibilities for their responses to His Word. The Word of God is here (Revelation 3:20); God's voice is here. Has anyone heard His voice? He is knocking at people's door (Revelation 3:20), and can they hear? The competition has clearly come between God's voice and Satan's. Which frequency of the spiritual hearing has people set? The choices of spiritual hearing have wide-range options, and people may spoil themselves, from the lust to the loss of themselves in the worldly treasures, e.g., committing adultery relationship, stealing, forcing people against God's will, or slandering, to reject God's frequency.

Then the man bowed down and worshipped the LORD, saying, "Praise be to the LORD, the God of my master Abraham, who has not abandoned his kindness and faithfulness to my master. As for me, the LORD has led me on the journey to the house of my master's relatives."

(Genesis 24:26–27)

To choose what they want, people have to have direction and guidance from God to exercise their freedom, according to His voice, which is the Word of God. There are many factors that have affected their choices. These factors can be the lack of the understanding of God's Word, false teaching, false doctrine, false church, manipulation, threats, depravity, or disparity. Are those people under this kind of situation to be blamed for making a wrong choice? No. God has not blamed them, for He has already known those who have really done wrong against people. God will send His angels, Holy Spirit, and His Good Samaritans (Luke 10:25-37) to save the oppressed, weak, and the suppressed. The spiritual warfare is real since the patriarch time, e.g., the deception of Eve and Adam (Genesis 3), and it has been existed since the creation of human being.

The complexities of the satanic natures (Romans 1:18-32) are far more than one understands or can anticipate. The reasons to do wrong may never be comprehended, or even psychologists and psychiatrists may never understand why people would choose to do wrong. We shall not judge others (Matthew 7:5) when they are doing wrong, for we are not in "their shoes", having no understanding of their situations. But we should help them to get out of their distress that is to free them from the darkness (Acts 18:11; 2 Corinthians 5:11; James 3:13-18).

In the book of Romans, 1:18-32, Apostle Paul has spelled out the sinful human natures, or Satan, and some of them are quite serious to the point that the sins, such as the first homicide of Cain killing Abel (Genesis 4), may bring them to jail in our time, the twenty-first century. Rescuing people from the darkness is actually the calling and the responsibility of His believers, such as Matthew 28:18-20.

To him who is able to keep you from falling
and to present you before his glorious
presence without fault and with great
joy—to the only God our Savior be glory,
majesty, power and authority, through Jesus
Christ our Lord, before all ages, now
and forevermore! Amen.

(Jude 1:24-25)

Making His creation, the Creator God neither calls upon His people to destroy each other, nor picks up the judgment rod to beat up each other or to kill each other. If His will was to destroy His creatures, e.g., people, why has He spent six days to build people's basic needs and to make sure that they have all the needs on this planet Earth in the first place? Why did He just allow the earth flying around the universe? And, if He knew that He was going to destroy His own creatures, then why did He build the protections, such as the ozone layer, for His planet Earth? The earth has not been flown out from its course or its path, for God's hand is still holding on the earth. Otherwise, the Earth might be like other asteroid, bumping to other planet and causing explosion in the universe. God never destroys us, for He loves us (1 John 4:19). God has revealed His love onto His creation (Genesis 41:25; Luke 10:21; 1 Peter 1:13).

God loves us, and our response is to love Him back; that is the First Commandment (Deuteronomy 6:5; Mark 12:29-30). Have people obeyed this commandment? The problems of people unable to obey this commandment are: (1) Some people think that God is not real, (2) Some people cannot accept the non-physicality of God, (3) Some put themselves above God, (4) Some think that God cannot see their wrong doing, (5) Some cannot accept the spirituality of God, (6) Problems in some of the His churches, e.g., abuse, have caused the believers to reject Him, or (7) Some refuse to obey God's commandments, for the commandments do not allow them to do their own wills. If people refuse to respond to God's revelation, for whatever their reasons may be, are people wrong? People's responses, which are the results or the consequence of their responses, either satanic or godly, have manifested in their societies. Only the godly responses can please God, not pleasing men (1 Thessalonians 2:4), but saving lives (Luke 10:25-37).

The city does not need the sun or the moon
to shine on it, for the glory of God gives it
light, and the Lamb is its lamp.

(Revelation 21:23)

VII.
CAUSES AND EFFECTS OF PEOPLE'S RESPONSES

"He made the earth by his power; he founded the world by his wisdom and stretched out the heavens by his understanding" (Jeremiah 51:15).

As revealing Himself to His creatures in the past, God has continually revealed Himself in the present, never stopping His revelation, which continues to the future, to His creatures. If people neglect, ignore, or walk away from His instructions, who will be the one to take the blame? God's instructions are our protections and defense, e.g., the Ten Commandments (Deuteronomy 5), in which God has shown His love to us. For instance, one of the Ten Commandments says that "You shall not kill." If one responded not to obey this commandment, then this person might plan to kill other or might experiment the killing of other. However, this instruction here is God tells people not to think about the killing of other, not to plan to kill other, or not to have the desire to kill other, including not to carrying out the act of killing other.

God does not allow people to go into the stage of the killing act, for people should immediately stop the killing desire or thought in their heart, mind, and their soul. But, if one responded to one's killing desire, it could be deadly, producing a very bad side effect. Satan (Matthew 4:10; Mark 8:33), dwelling into an individual, has driven to kill and to destroy others due to the hatred, misunderstanding, or other personal reason, e.g., Hitler. Have people seen the causes and effects of one's response to a satanic thought?

When Christ came as high priest of the good things that are already here, he went through the greater and more perfect tabernacle that is not man-made, that is to say, not a part of this creation.

(Hebrews 9:11)

Having many innocent killings, from international to domestic, there have been many innocent victims. For instance, Mexican drug lords' killings have reached to, at least, 50,000 people today since 2006. The causes and effects of people's responses to a satanic thought have much to do their views of God. Never destroying what He creates, God has made the promise, in which He has said in the Word of God. He never gives anyone, including His anointed ones, to have a license to kill, to have a law to destroy, or to have a rule or regulation to get rid of others.

Consequently, we rationalize that as He has sent His Begotten Son died for us to pay for our sins once for all (Hebrews 9:26; 1 John 2:2), what make people think that He is going to turn around to destroy us? Would one's response to Him be wrong that has caused the destruction of His creation, e.g., human being or His planet Earth?

This is what the LORD says, he who appoints the sun to shine by day, who decrees the moon and stars to shine by night, who stirs up the sea so that its waves roar—the LORD Almighty is his name: "Only if these decrees vanish from my sight," declares the LORD, "will the descendants of Israel ever cease to be a nation before me."

(Jeremiah 31:35-36)

When people have problems, they usually blame God. After reading the war between Japan and China several years ago, I have learned more facts. One of the facts is the other nations have refused to step in to stop the brutal, non-sense killing of the innocent Chinese and the invasion and illegal occupation in China. It is not until Japan attacked the Pearl Harbor without a declaration of war. Thus, it all comes down to people's responses.

What if the other nations responded to the Japanese aggressive invasion in China sooner, then more innocent Chinese could have been saved. What if the other nations responded to the Hitler's killing of Jews sooner, then more innocent Jews could have been saved. It is all about people's responses, and if people respond in a godly manner, then people can save the distress, weak, and the oppressed. People can indeed save life, like the Good Samaritan (Luke 10: 25-37).

The creation waits in eager expectation
for the sons of God to be revealed. For the
creation was subjected to frustration, not by
its own choice, but by the will of the one
who subjected it, in hope that the creation
itself will be liberated from its bondage to
decay and brought into the glorious freedom
of the children of God.

(Romans 8:19-21)

Do not blame God if terrible thing happens. God has given people the freedom to choose and to act. Human choices are sometimes complicated, being influenced by the politics, economy, prejudice, race, society, or spiritual situations. If God has not forced anyone, such as seven billions of the world population, becoming Christians, people should not blame Him for anything, such as disease (Matthew 4:23), distress (Matthew 24:21), disappointment (Matthew 19:22), or death (Genesis 4).

Back to the Old Testament, Moses' sister, Miriam, and brother, Aaron, both listened to their people, making the Golden Calf while Moses was still praying on the top of the mountain (Exodus 32:1). Miriam and Aaron also received the teaching from God, as both of them being let astray from Him upon the temptation. Their responses have failed God and have led them to the God's punishment (Deuteronomy 9:7).

Moses has repented and apologized for the wrong doing of his siblings and people. God has taught them again. Their mistakes are also documented in the Word of God, e.g., the books of Exodus and Deuteronomy. This lesson is much more than the problem of worshipping idol or the disobedience of the First Commandment (Deuteronomy 6:5), but the most important thing is Moses' sister and brother have known God, and they were supposed to teach their people to walk right with God. However, they have misled their people and have built the Golden Calf against Him, and that made this mistake is so severe, for they have been anointed (the book of Exodus).

then hear from heaven, your dwelling place,

and do whatever the foreigner asks of you,

so that all the peoples of the earth may

know your name and fear you, as do your

own people Israel, and may know that this

house I have built bears your Name.

(1 Kings 8:43)

✝

Disasters (Exodus 19:16), diseases (Matthew 4:23), disappointments (Luke 18:23), or distresses (Romans 2:9) are not new to the human history, and the human responses have been improving throughout the years in terms of preventions. The disasters, such as earthquake (1 King 19:11-12), hail (Joshua 10:11), or thunderstorm (Isaiah 30:30), are not only happened in the year of 2000 or in the year of 2012, but they have been existed many centuries ago. As the matter of the fact, the earthquakes (1 King 19:11; Ezekiel 38:19) have documented back in the Word of God, including the storms (Psalm 107:25; Isaiah 4:6); for instance, the Lord Jesus Christ has calmed the storm, as he said to his disciples (Luke 8:24).

Moreover, the Lord Jesus Christ has taught his audiences that when the sky was red, they learned that the storm was coming (Matthew 16:2-3). The Lord has also acknowledged the diseases, which were not new in the Word of God, such as Matthew 4:23. The diseases and disasters have not been new in the human history, and why do the human beings, God's creatures, blame Him or His believers in the twenty-first century? When God has given His wisdom to us to anticipate problems, people should not blame anyone, but they should seek the preventive measures to protect themselves, such as the online sources, e.g., www.cdc.gov or www. noaa.gov .

Nowadays, in U.S.A. we have the Food and Drug Administration (FDA), and it has been existed for decades. Some nations do not have one even onto this day. We did not had one until our nation finally had a government several hundred years ago, so now we have an administration, called FDA, in short. The FDA continues to improve and to expand their services, such as teaching people how to read food label in which it is one of the preventive measures to educate people, how to eat right and how to calculate calories, to help people to live in a healthy condition, and to keep the cost of the health care insurance down.

The preventive measures, lessons, warnings, rules, regulations, and the teachings of the FDA are just like the Good News, the Scriptures, the Gospel, or the Word of God, which provides the preventive measures, lessons, warnings, rules, regulations, and the teachings to His creatures, people.

The God who made the world and
everything in it is the Lord of heaven and
earth and does not live in temples
built by hands.

(Acts 17:24)

Disappointments and distresses that people face every day have not new in their world. The satanic forces do exist in our midst. For instance, the manual of the DMV, Department of Motor Vehicles, has already said that a driver has to stop in front of the red light. But this driver chose to challenge the red light and the speed of his car, and now his prideful, stubborn heart refused to stop in front of the red light, and car accident occurred . . . Can the car accident be avoidable? Yes.

To be godly is to be humble to experience God's presence, in the midst of our lives. If the driver acted godly, he could have avoided the accident. For every single act that we, people, are doing has the consequence. If our acts are godly, we save people. If one's act is a destructive one, e.g., getting rid of people, one produces one's victims. It has been on the news about the killings of the drug wars in Mexico, which have been there for several years, and the Mexican government has not been able to stop the killings. The distress of those who have lived there is unimaginable, and even our government has issued the travel warning, not to travel there, for the violence of drug wars is real and overwhelmed. Are we going to blame God for the deaths? No. It is not what God is doing there. But bad people have chosen to do Satan's way to destroy the households, to kill people, and to disrupt people's livelihoods. It is all about the responses of human beings. What if they have known God, they would not have chosen to destroy His creatures, people.

How many are your works, O LORD! In
wisdom you made them all; the earth is full
of your creatures.

(Psalm 104:24)

VIII.
THE REVELATION OF GOD

"The revelation of Jesus Christ, which God gave him to show his servants what must soon take place. He made it known by sending his angel to his servant John, who testifies to everything he saw—that is, the word of God and the testimony of Jesus Christ" (Revelation 1:1-2).

The Word of God has been sealed and has been closed several thousand years ago (Revelation 22:18-19). God has revealed Himself since the creation of the heaven and earth (Genesis 35:7; 2 King 8:10; Romans 16:26). His Word has been read by billions of people, either believers or non-believers. Many people have tried to prove God's Word was inaccurate or false. But, after all, the Holy Spirit which dwells in the Word of God has changed and transformed people (1 Timothy 4:5), who have tried to challenge His Word and existence. These former challengers, e.g., Apostle Paul (Acts 9), have become missionary people, preachers, ministers, and directors of missionaries. God has the power to change and to transform the prideful stubborn heart, and He is still alive and well today.

The Word of God has taught people to be like Him (Romans 13:13-14), but not against His creatures or against Himself. His Word never means to hurt people or to harm anyone, but it means to help people to live in a safe and sound environment. God has created His creatures and has given them assignments to take good care of His planet Earth, as stewards and stewardesses (Genesis 1:26-27). God never assigns anyone to destroy other creation, from human beings to His environment. His Word has clearly spelled out the measures, which are His commandments and instructions, to help His people to take good care of the earth, from spiritual issues to earthly matters.

I tell you the truth, this generation will
certainly not pass away until all these things
have happened. Heaven and earth will pass
away, but my words will never pass away.

(Matthew 24:34-35)

God has revealed His instructions to His people, as His people carrying out the assignment, according to His instructions (Joshua 23:6; Revelation 22:7), like the faithful moon (Psalm 89:37). The Word of God has revealed His wisdom which is given to His people how to handle the earthly and spiritual matters (Romans 13:13; James 3:13-18), having expounded the rules and regulations according to His will, to keep us safe and to prevent us astray from God. He has set up the administrative measures how to build His church, from an initiation to the maintenance, such as the books of Corinthians, not just a physical structure but also a spiritual one, which is His creature, an human being that is a God's temple or a temple of the Holy Spirit (1 Corinthians 3:16-17).

The initiation of His temple is just one step, after many steps, such as an opportunity of hearing Gospel (Acts 18:11; 1Timothy 4:13), have occurred. God has revealed all these steps in His Word, such as the Lord Jesus Christ preaching on the Mount (Matthew 5). By the hearing of His Word, God has rewarded to His people (Matthew 11:15; Hebrews 3:15), and this step has been ongoing since the Old Testament.

The teaching and preaching of His Word have provided an opportunity to allow His instructions to be revealed to people, and these steps have neither interfered nor stopped by anyone or any force (Deuteronomy 31:22; Matthew 24:14). His Word is continually revealed to people, either believers or non-believers, to this day. To make His Word known to people is one of the commandments, such as the Great Commission Commandment (Matthew 28:18-20). God has never stopped saving people. Despite of the spiritual hearing, people may not tune into the hearing of His Word, but there will be time that they will hear and acknowledge His instructions (Matthew 13:9).

The angel said to me, "These words are trustworthy and true. The Lord, the God of the spirits of the prophets, sent his angel to show his servants the things that must soon take place. "Behold, I am coming soon! Blessed is he who keeps the words of the prophecy in this book."

(Revelation 22: 6-7)

As studying the first book of the Scriptures, Genesis, people will learn about the human failures, such as the deception and killing (Genesis 3-4). The weakness and sinful human natures have already noticed in the first book, Genesis. The sins, nowadays, may also call crimes, e.g., homicide and robbery, which have already been present thousands and thousands years ago. The deception, the first disobedience to God's instructions, of Eve and Adam is happened in the Garden of Eden (Genesis 3). It also stirs up the first God's noticeable anger back in the patriarch time, for people are so easy being let astray from His instructions. The weak and sinful natures have not been new to our history.

The first capital sin, or crime, was done by Cain, who has killed his own brother, Abel (Genesis 4), as we have acknowledged today, a capital murder. It is caused by the jealousy, which is the envious act that leads to the killing of other. Has this kind of killing act stopped today? No. The sinful human natures have been existed (Romans 1:18-32). Sinners may have whatever reason to commit different kinds of sins, such as sexually immorality, swindling, raping, stealing, slandering, or killing, which have been warned and taught by God that His people shall not commit sin, and some of the sins are the crimes of the twenty-first century.

The LORD saw how great man's wickedness on the earth had become, and that every inclination of the thoughts of his heart was only evil all the time. The LORD was grieved that he had made man on the earth, and his heart was filled with pain.

(Genesis 6:5-6)

People have to acknowledge God's presence and His will and to accept His Begotten Son, the Lord Jesus Christ, as their personal Savior (Luke 10:21; Romans 5:11). God reveals all His promises and instructions to His people. If people refuse to accept Him, can they blame Him for their problems when they could not even become His believers? Or what if the situation was turning around, God became a dictator, who forced His creatures, people, to accept Him as their personal God, and what would happen then? Did we need to believe and to read His Word daily? Did we have to care about His ministry? Did we have to go to His church since we were forced to accept Him? Did we need to have a church or a seminary education? Did we need to believe the Holy Spirit? Did we have to pray in Christ's name? Or everyone just lined up in the stadium to worship God, like the North Koreans worshipping their leaders.

However, has God gone ahead to force people to accept Him as their personal God? If the answer was "yes," then Christ did not need to die for us. Perhaps, Israel did not have to crucify their own Yahweh, their own Messiah. But, the truth is God has never forced anyone to accept Him. He, instead, does send His Beloved Son Jesus Christ to die for us to pay for our sins once for all (Romans 3:30; 5:8). Only Satan (Genesis 2:9; Matthew 12:26; Mark 4:15) is always deceiving, cheating, swindling, stealing, slandering, killing, or lying in which these are his characters (Romans 1:18-32). There are a lot of alternatives that God could do and can do. All these times, God has never given up people. When we look up to the sky today, it is still there.

He raises the poor from the dust and lifts the
needy from the ash heap; he seats them with
princes and has them inherit a throne of
honor. "For the foundations of the earth are
the LORD's; upon them he
has set the world.

(1 Samuel 2:8)

Waking up every morning, we can still walk on the ground, which is still attached on the earth. In the universe there have been explosions. After the explosion, a new star, or a new planet, is born, and this kind of scenario is not new to our cosmic event. If the explosion happened to our planet Earth, what would people expect then? Why has our earth, itself, not had any explosion yet? Today we can still walk on the ground. It is because God has made His promises to protect His creatures, us, and He continues to reveal His instructions to us, such as the books of Genesis and Revelation.

Remember your servants Abraham, Isaac
and Israel, to whom you swore by your
own self: 'I will make your descendants
as numerous as the stars in the sky and I
will give your descendants all this land
I promised them, and it will be their
inheritance forever.'

(Exodus 32:13)

IX.
HUMAN RELATIONSHIP WITH THE CREATOR GOD

"Now we know that if the earthly tent we live in is destroyed, we have a building from God, an eternal house in heaven, not built by human hands" (2 Corinthians 5:1).

God is the Creator God (1 Peter 4:19), spelling out His relation with His creatures, people, starting at the first book, Genesis, of the Word of God. His divine wisdom, to His creation, which is heaven and earth, including all living things, has been demonstrated the presence of His divine Almighty power that has been existed and has been proven in our universe, such as the book of Exodus. When people wake up, having problem, e.g., disaster, can they blame God? No. God is the Creator God. He will never destroy what He creates. For instance, the extreme weather patterns are the illustrations of the poor stewardship secondary to the adverse side effects of the poor maintenances of the planet Earth, such as the industrialization and deforestation.

Continually teaching people to take good care of His planet Earth, God gives wisdom to people, who then have different kind of expertise to solve the earthly problems. Have people listened to those experts? God has never taught people how to pollute the environment, the planet Earth? For instance, if people know how to make the chemicals, then they should know how to provide the aftercare of the by-products of their chemicals, called the chemical wastes. If they do not know how to do the aftercare of the waste, then they should not make the chemicals in the first place.

This is the account of the heavens and
the earth when they were created. When
the LORD God made the earth and the
heavens—and no shrub of the field had yet
appeared on the earth and no plant of the
field had yet sprung up, for the LORD God
had not sent rain on the earth and there was
no man to work the ground, but streams
came up from the earth and watered the
whole surface of the ground—the LORD
God formed the man from the dust of the
ground and breathed into his nostrils the
breath of life, and the man became
a living being.

(Genesis 2:4-7)

Now the pollutants are accumulated in a rapid pace that the extra molecules, such as carbon dioxide, are either storing in our water, e.g., ocean, or our sky, the stratosphere. For instance, the pollutants come down to the food chains, such as vegetables or meats, which may be cows, pigs, or chickens. The food that people have may harm the body for the presence of the pollutants, such as thousands and thousands of fishes being recently found dead on the coast of South America.

Teaching His creatures, people, to love Him and to respect His creations, God always encourages people to have good relationship with Him, but not forcing them to accept Him as their personal God. He also teaches people how to take good care of His Earth, such as nurturing His land and water in the book of Leviticus. In the Old Testament, God has given His divine wisdom to people how to be good stewards and stewardesses, e.g., the books of Exodus and Deuteronomy. It is not about people in our time, the twenty-first century, have to do the exact things back to the patriarch time; but instead, people in our time have to learn the foundation of the knowledge, which is His instructions, of how to take good care of the planet Earth, and they should integrate the knowledge with the modern technologies, e.g., solar energy. God has revealed His wisdom to people; however, because of the prideful and stubborn hearts, people have chosen their own ways. When the disaster comes, people blame God.

What agreement is there between the temple of God and idols? For we are the temple of the living God. As God has said: "I will live with them and walk among them, and I will be their God, and they will be my people."

(2 Corinthians 6:16)

Please do not blame God, for people have known His wisdom to solve the earthly problems. It is their disobedience to His instructions that have caused the problems. God has already given wisdom to people, who have the expertise to preserve the resources or to protect the environment, such as the engineer. For instance, a doctor told his patient not to smoke, or he might have cardio-vascular diseases. His patient refused to obey the instruction, and he would be at his own risk. Can this patient blame his doctor for the diseases? No. And the same scenario does apply. God has released His instructions, the Scriptures, beforehand, and people should obey His instructions, for there is only one planet Earth to which God has created for His creatures (2 Corinthians 12:9), which are us, called people (Genesis 2).

God reveals His image to people, so people will have His images (Colossians 1:15; 3:10). God reveals His wisdom to people, so people shall have His wisdom. God gives His instructions to people, so people become good stewards and good stewardesses (Matthew 24:45-46; Colossians 1:25). Therefore, His creatures, people, should learn how to take good care of themselves and of others, and they shall be safe and sufficient (Matthew 25:23) on this planet Earth.

As continually worshiping God, we will have His protection in which it leads us to walk with Him through the Lord Jesus Christ (2 Thessalonians 3:3; 1 Corinthians 10:13). God has mentioned the importance of the relationship with Him many times, such as obeying His instructions (John 14:15; Revelation 14:12), in His Word, for He is Holy (Revelation 4:8), righteous (Romans 1:17), and just (2 Thessalonians 1:6).

His instructions, e.g., the Ten Commandments (Deuteronomy 5), are for our protection, discernments, and our defense, helping us to fend off the troubles. For instance, if the nurse said to her patient that she had to wear the gloves before the change of the dressing, but her patient disobeyed the instruction. And one week later, the patient returned to the clinic for the infected wound due to not wearing gloves to cleanse the wound. It is just like God has revealed His instructions to people, but people have chosen to disobey. After they have known His instructions, why do people blame Him for their problems when they refuse to obey His Word?

Your heart became proud on account of your beauty, and you corrupted your wisdom because of your splendor. So I threw you to the earth; I made a spectacle of you before kings.

(Ezekiel 28:17)

People's failures are caused by the disobedience to His instructions and are disrupted by the lack of the relationship with the Creator God. The Word of God is not saying that Satan cannot kill people physically, spiritually, financially, politically, or environmentally, but it says that Satan cannot save or revive people spiritually, for God has the ministry of the reconciliation (2 Corinthians 5:18), which has the power and the wisdom of God that will save the world through the Lord Jesus Christ. Besides, God's presence is omnipresent; God's knowledge is omniscient; God's power is omnipotent. While we are still living, our appreciations of God's mercy and grace have to take place, as the manifestation of our relationship with Him.

"And we have seen and testify that the Father has sent his Son to be the Savior of the world" (1 John 4:14).

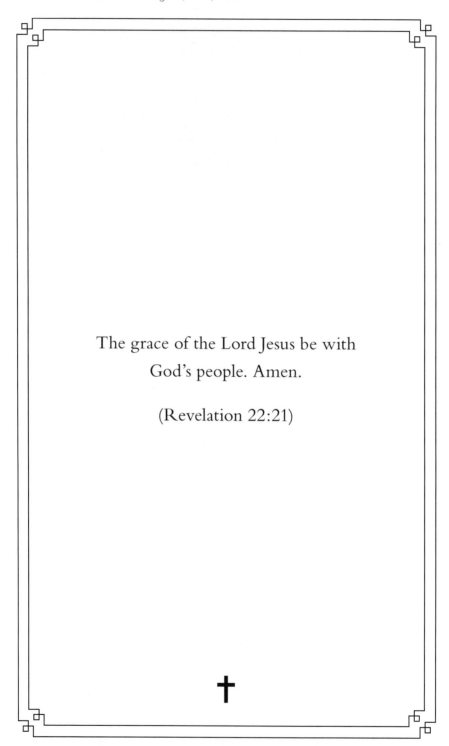

The grace of the Lord Jesus be with
God's people. Amen.

(Revelation 22:21)

✝

X.
APPENDIX I: THE PREVIEW FOR THE NEXT BOOK

LOVING GOD: Our Creator God, Volume 1

- in April, 2013.
- This book is going to focus: (1) The Creator God, (2) God's Attributes, and (3) God's Ministry.

APPENDIX II: PRAISE MUSIC

A. No One Dies in Jesus Name (Key signature: C)

Intro: C///G///Am///

Verse 1:

C

Let us humble,

G

so no one dies

Am

in Jesus name.

C

Let us yield

G

one step, so

Am

people have space

C

to stand, so

G

no one dies

Am

in Jesus name.

(Play Intro. Then repeat Verse 1)

G   Am   C

No one dies in Jesus Name. (2 times) Amen.

B. Let Your Light Shine (Key Signature: G)

Intro: G///C///A///Em///

Verse 1

G   C   A   Em

In darkness, whisper the help through the air,

      C   Am

hear the sound of hatred.

Chorus:

G   Dm   C

Only in the name of the Lord Jesus,

A   C   G

find my Savior, who looks upon me.

Am   C   Em

Provide comfort and trust.

(G///C///A///Em///)

Verse 2

In lonesome place, cry out for direction.

Fear from within.

Chorus:

Only in the name of the Lord Jesus,

find my Savior, who looks upon me.

Provide comfort and trust.

(G///C///A///Em///)

Pre-Chorus:

G   A   C

(Lord Jesus, O Lord Jesus)

Let your light shine upon me.

G   C   Dm

(Lord Jesus, O Lord Jesus)

Let the darkness be brighten up

G   C   A

(Lord Jesus, O Lord Jesus)

Let your name be my protector,

Dm   C   G

(Lord Jesus, O Lord Jesus)

only in the name of Jesus.

A   C   A   C

(Lord Jesus, O Lord Jesus) (Lord Jesus, O Lord Jesus)

Let your light shine upon me. (Lord Jesus, O Lord Jesus)

C

Amen.

C. 2012 Graduates (Key Signature: G)

Intro: G///C///Am///Dm///

Verse 1:

G   C   Am   Dm   Am

A journey is like a mountain hike, a fall, a bump, a scrape,

Dm

and a cut.

G   C   Am   Dm   Am

A journey is like a river sail, a rise, a drop, a toss, and a

Dm

stop.

Chorus:

G   C   Am   Dm   C

Thanks for the Lord Jesus for the journey in your garden.

G   Dm   G   C   Am   Dm

Congratulate 2-0-1-2 GRADUATES.

(G////C////Am////Dm////)

Verse 2:

A journey is like a stroll, a breeze, a leisure, a pleasure, and a step.

A journey is like a car ride, a turn, a hit, a fix, and a fuel.

Chorus:

Thanks for the Lord Jesus for the journey in your garden.

Congratulate 2-0-1-2 GRADUATES.

(Intro: G////C////Am////Dm////)

Verse 3:

A journey advances to graduation, a look back, a smile, a pain, and a memory.

A journey gives thanks to our seminary for leading us to completion.

Chorus:

Thanks for the Lord Jesus for the journey in your garden.

Congratulate 2-0-1-2 GRADUATES.

D. One Nation under God (Key Signature: C)

Intro: C////G////Am////

Verse 1:

    C   G

Coming from every side,

Am   D   Em

rest in a precious land,

      G7

a land of freedom,

D   C   G

under God's sight. (Intro: C////G////Am////)

Chorus:

C   G   Am

One nation under God

D   Em   C   G

is only by Spirit, His, and by will, ours.

Verse 2:

    C   G

Speaking different tongue,

Am   D   Em

bear in precious culture,

a land of freedom,

under God's law. (Intro: C////G////Am////)

Chorus:

One nation under God

is only by Spirit, His, and by will, ours.

Verse 3:

C   G

Having color,

Am   D   Em

build a sweet home,

a land of freedom,

under God's sky. (Intro: C////G////Am////)

Chorus:

One nation under God

is only by Spirit, His, and by will, ours.

Verse 4:

C   G

Letting astray,

Am   D   Em

return to His church,

a land of freedom,

under God's will. (Intro: C////G////Am////)

Chorus:

One nation under God

is only by Spirit, His, and by will, ours.